OPUS POSTHUMOUS
AND OTHER POEMS

OPUS POSTHUMOUS
AND OTHER POEMS

DAVID R. SLAVITT

Louisiana State University Press
Baton Rouge

Published by Louisiana State University Press
lsupress.org

LSU Press Paperback Original

Designer: Barbara Neely Bourgoyne
Typeface: Arno Pro

From the Fragrant East was previously published by Miracolo Press. "Two Sonnets," by
Louise Labé; "Villanesque," by Jacques Grévin; "A Fountain," by Philippe Desportes;
"Nightingales," by Bernard de Ventadorn; and "Sonnet," by Étienne Jodelle, previously
appeared in *Poésies.*

Cover illustration: Unsplash.com/Bernard Hermant; 3D typographic render by
Brad Michael Bourgoyne

Library of Congress Cataloging-in-Publication Data
Names: Slavitt, David R., 1935– author.
Title: Opus posthumous and other poems / David R. Slavitt.
Description: Baton Rouge : Louisiana State University Press, [2021]
Identifiers: LCCN 2021004098 (print) | LCCN 2021004099 (ebook) |
    ISBN 978-0-8071-7566-8 (paperback) | ISBN 978-0-8071-7642-9 (pdf) |
    ISBN 978-0-8071-7643-6 (epub)
Subjects: LCGFT: Poetry.
Classification: LCC PS3569.L3 O68 2021 (print) | LCC PS3569.L3 (ebook) |
    DDC 811/.54—dc23
LC record available at https://lccn.loc.gov/2021004098
LC ebook record available at https://lccn.loc.gov/2021004099

For Janet

CONTENTS

TRANSLATIONS, TRANSFORMATIONS, ADAPTATIONS

OPUS POSTHUMOUS
AND OTHER POEMS

PYRE

Books can burn, as all barbarians know,
and in wars of ideas this can be a convenience,
but it never crosses their empty minds that although
paper burns, the words and their intents
do not climb on the gray smoke into the sky
to enlighten and entertain birds flying by.

They soar higher and higher from the ground
where the letters separate and then fly free
or recombine to make new words that sound
strange and refer to things we cannot see
or even imagine, never having learned
to read from books that have been destroyed or burned.

It turns out not infrequently that they
are the ones that matter most and are etched into
our lives with time's acid so that they stay
in print at least as long as our bodies do.
They may diminish to mere motes in the air,
but dispersed, they leave their traces everywhere,

which, after all, is what books ought to do,
exhaling oxygen for us, like the trees,
that we need to breathe. Assuming it is true
that nothing is ever lost, any random breeze
can bring back the ancients' wisdom with a slight
trace of Pergamon's library still in flight.

Those summer midges that swarm and seem to dance
in the air above us are educated, for they
know all that they need to know: the chance
collisions of surviving letters say
words we may not know but can take in
by breathing or through a tingling of the skin.

MORNING FOG

You cannot see the sea, or rather say
you cannot see the demarcation of sea
and sky in a morning fog that will soon burn off.
Meanwhile you take the line of foam at your feet
the spent waves leave along the sand
as the only horizon. Beyond it there is a gray
in which nothing proclaims itself. That nothing
is, for the time being, everything

you know or could remember, if you were keener,
of the whole world, the welkin, the universe,
in which your senses say you are the center.
You have sometimes thought this but never dared
say such a thing aloud to anyone else
of the fog's foible that is your secret to keep.

SPACES

In the spaces between the words, we once lived
and breathed in safety, for they could not deceive,
distort the world, or make us doubt our moods
or likes and dislikes that prompt fights and flights.
We trusted them and their simplicity.
Words with their complications are distracting,
making us question what we thought we knew.
Grief and love are not so much beyond
words as prior to them with their mute
truths: the spaces are precious fragments, shards
of what remains of the unblemished whiteness
with which we began and begin and again begin.

INTERMEDIATE ENGLISH—G. STEIN

Instead of il signor Giaccomo in Trieste,
just for fun let it be Paris, let
Mme Gertrude teach at Berlitz. She is
a "native English speaker" (technically, yes)
and students come to learn to write business letters:
how many days, how many days are there in it,
and what is the rate of interest you pay? You pay
attention, too, to the rose that remains a rose
throughout its many grammatical permutations,
bud to bloom to blown, and noun or verb,
for the roses arose in rows. My word! (It is
my word: it registers now as a trademark.)
The pigeon, too, on the grass (Alas! Oh woe!)
is better known—I cannot imagine why—
than a magpie that can fly high in the sky.

GROCERIES

Cloudy nights obscure them, or light pollution,
and the stars disappear. But we can get new ones
at Star Market. The children know it's nonsense,
even as they see its sense. The balance
dizzies them but not too much.

                              Waldbaum's,
Safeway, and Food Emporium do not offer
such food for thought and cannot restock the sky.
The Magi shopped at Star for butter, milk,
a dozen eggs, maybe. And also myrrh.

OPUS POSTHUMOUS

Buried alive, I scratch at the coffin lid
not anymore to get help but to let them know,
if by some chance they should someday exhume me,
what a deplorable death I had.
                               Will they wonder
whose fault it was, whose inattention
(or was it an act of cruelty?) caused this?
It will not matter. It does not matter now,
but it passes the time as I use up the air.

TOLEDO MUD HENS

This inky-thinky stuff? Show off!
Wow, does he know a lot!
Couldn't have said it better myself.
Or as well.
Should I be jealous? Am I not beyond that?
Is it enough to know how little I know
and how slapdash?
No one I can think of
admits any of this. Win or lose,
they won't even let on that it's a game,
rough and with lots of concussions
as they slap their foreheads again and again.
Even in the stands (it's a sparse crowd:
this is the minor league)
fans can be injured.
A line drive can do you in anytime.

OUTSIDE

Rain batters the skylight, and trees outside
in the wind huddle together: I am warm
and dry in here, snug but not smug.
The storm intensifies with bolts of lightning
and, after an interval I count off,
thunder. But Zeus is long dead and Jove
and, knowing that none of this has any meaning,
I must confront and admit my helplessness.

From randomness I hide under blankets
of far-fetched, outdated metaphors
from the world's childhood and mine, too,
and am dumbfounded after this demonstration
of irrational power. It will pass away
or I will—and I don't have the choice.

COBRAS

The snake rises up from the charmer's basket,
extends its hood, and moves from left to right,
graceful in its ancient dance: spectators
admire and are afraid. Without the fear,
the performance is trivialized, no longer a matter
of life and death and much less entertaining.

The acetylcholine receptors of the mongoose
make it almost immune to snake venom—
unfair, but so is the venom. Let the cobras
be poets, in a trope that makes mongooses
professors and critics, very fast and thick-skinned,
encountering poems that ought to be dangerous.
When young, mongooses may have been in peril
but less and less and then not anymore.

STAFFAGE

The paintings are never about them, incidentals,
standing under a tree or out on a hillside
as punctuation or to suggest scale.
But let us suppose they know this and are content.
Reversing everything so the lavish landscape
is not a mere surround but their dream. They could be
the painter's invitation to our attention
to pause however briefly. Off in their corner,
as if they were shy or hiding, they are too small
to bear prolonged scrutiny. Even so,
go for a walk, look up and around, and see
how we are all small, no matter what
we imagine and most of the time take for granted:
almost never are we the subjects of paintings.

STONE

Amichai was lucky to find that stone
with *Amen* written on it: meaning glittered
as light from a brilliant-cut diamond. Mine,
oddly shaped, dull brown, says nothing,

but I picked it up at Masada, thinking maybe
for my parents' gravestone or mine. On my desk
impervious to any interpretation,
whatever it may remember it keeps to itself.

COHORT

Almost always of people older than me,
the obits used to reassure and amuse
but then less and less.
Lots of these high achievers are younger now
than me, often by decades.
I am pleased to have outlasted them.
But also less and less.

CASINO

With flashing lights and beeping noises, the whole
shebing-bang-bong is also a garish temple
to Fortune, whose intercession we seek,
having been forced at last to admit her power.

But the metaphor breaks down as they all do.
The stakes are higher here because we bet
our lives on every play. No golf, no pool
or buffets distract us as we check or raise

doggedly on the dismal hands we are dealt.
Over time, the odds against us mount
as even the dollar-table players know,
who sit in their hellish semicircle and count

cards. We are in denial. Chips come and go—
not mere money in disguise but time
and consciousness itself. We do not expect
to win, but we can hope to lose more slowly.

REAL ESTATE

May I, enjoying long life and still seeing, enter old age
as if it were the house I live in.
—*Rig Veda*, Mandala I, hymn 117

What makes your house a comfort is how it has turned
invisible, so that you can take it for granted.
Without having to look, you know the rooms,
their doors and the light switches, furniture, objects
and can move your hands and feet in pitch darkness
with confidence. Your body, though, is not
the one you used to have or might like now,
but this, its address always in the present.

The neighborhood deteriorates and friends
move away. This troubles you but less
as you walk the same sidewalks every day
and feel with the soles of your feet the paving stones'
acknowledgment that you've earned after all these years
and from which you take whatever strength you can.

WHAT THE GIBBONS SING

From high in the trees at dawn they vocalize,
and naturalists below are filled with wonder
as all the gibbons sing, pouring out their hearts:
Want to fuck? I'm hungry! I am afraid.
Nice day. Some of their songs are not weighted
with meanings but float as they do from one tree
to the next through the still, cool morning air.
They live in the garden from which Adam and Eve
were banished, and we look up, both amazed
and also nostalgic. For them there is neither past
nor future, which our verbs nicely distinguish.
Without words they negotiate space and time
with an agile balance we barely recognize.

AMERICA

God bless mairzy doats
land of salagadoola,
stand beside her
and chi-lawa kook-a la goombah
through the night
with a bah-da-rah-da-boom-foo-dee-ay
from above.

From the hibbidy-gits
to the chickory-chick
to the ting tang walla walla bing bang
white with foam,
God bless my filla-da-gush, filla-ma-rusha,
my chi-baba, chi-wawa, sweet home.

GORILLAS

Because they are huge, we love them and think they're cute—
King Kong and the real ones, who are endangered,
so it is only right that they should be
preserved—with a preserve in which to loll,

eat bananas, and pick one another's fleas
in peace. Who can object to such Goodall
goodness? Of course, they had to remove the Pygmies,
or the Twa as they're called, forced out on a trail of tears

to somewhere else in Uganda. But who cares?
They are mere human beings, unappealing,
backward hunter-gatherers, spending their time
fending off hunger so that they do not carve

gewgaws from the wood of their local trees.
Our own species? But this is a disadvantage,
for we have learned over thousands of years
to kill one another routinely if not with glee.

THE WOODS

Beautiful maidens can turn in an instant into
something else, crones, with wickedness
in their hearts and ugly faces to match. All through
the woods there are such creatures or so we believed

in childhood. Later, grown up, we confronted
what was far more scary, that mute stones
speak and trees and the wild creatures, and always
the truth. Only human beings lie

or think to venture out of their groves and thickets
to the delusional towns that we have agreed on.
Stones do not change their position: they stay
fixed in their assertion of what is the case.

MAYFLIES

Their adults live a day. They cannot feed
and have no need of memory: for these
Ephemeroptera, there is only a vivid
now. But who can claim such concentration?

I can recover from my many years
glimpses of instants, seconds that add up—
because of my inattention . . . to what?
A few hours, not quite a mayfly's day.

PORLOCK

A silly, trivial name—like Peoria
or Poughkeepsie, with nothing but the alliteration
going for it. It has no features, is part
of the Exmoor National Park, but who cares?
Its Culbone Church is the smallest in England, but that
is irrelevant, too. The whole town is a joke
because of its person of business and his intrusion
that pissed Coleridge off. Naughty person!

Except that he is the world: Porlock is
alive and more important by any measure
than a dream of Xanadu and its sacred river.
The butt of the joke is Sam, who was not engaged
by the modest, sturdy truth of facticity.
The dialing code is 01643.

GREAT-GRANDSON

If we reach ages when you can remember me,
I may survive, but only as a blur.

Until then, you will be a figment
and I shall be a myth. Neither is true.

Too briefly, we may dance together
with our feet never quite touching the floor.

PSALM 127

No point, the psalmist says, in getting up early
or staying up late either if you are eating
the sourdough bread, ficelle, or boule of sorrow.
Consciousness is not your friend, or worse,
it hates itself and you, for who can distinguish
between his awareness of life and life itself?

The sun still shines in the sky across which birds
dart and swoop. Oceans rock in their beds.
Mostly, people enjoy this or take comfort
in the sights and sounds they wake to. But wisdom knows
to shut its eyelids again and delve in the darkness
for the truth behind the inviting prettiness.

FROST'S "MISGIVING"

It's a nice conceit: in the first three stanzas he
imagines that leaves have feelings and on the tree
long to be loosed by the cold and wind to fly
free in the air they have been waiting to try.

They flutter, even whirl a little, and then
may race across the ground a bit, but when
they've finished their brief excursion, if we may call
so short an adventure that, they find some wall

to huddle against and wait to rot. It would
be one of his better poems if only he could
have skipped the ending, his fear of death, his wan
hope for another life after he's gone.

He knew how to stop by the woods and leave it to us
to figure out what he meant without the fuss
of an explanation. Pour until the cup
is full but then stop. Know when to shut up.

ZOUAVES

Their aggressively wide, white, gauzy pantaloons
and broad scarlet sashes mock the precision
drills in which their stomping squads weave
patterns some Busby Berkley officer

dreamt up in a kif-graced moment. Algeria's
Zouaoua tribes dressed in such a way,
but without the suggestions Europeans took
from the farouche yet clearly feminine

extravagance: that resonant grace note
acknowledges the eroticism of killing.
The Janissaries' preposterous plumed hats
proclaim likewise a sinister, epicene

disregard of limit—but when they die,
their uniforms can serve as lamb chop frills
with which a *rôtisseur* will decorate
their dead meat displayed on the field's salver.

BIRTHDAYS

The day you were born? You can't remember that
or even the parties later with funny hats.
The world was unchanged, although you were in it now.
Call them a way to count. But looking backward
doesn't mean a thing. The other date
on the stonecutter's work order is all that matters,
and there is no point in making guesses.
You must show appreciation for relatives' calls
(not all will, and you can't help keeping track)
and endure the protracted awkwardness. You are both
relieved when you disconnect. These celebrations
have ossified to obligation, to nuisance,
a repetitive burden but better than nothing at all.

ANAPHORA

Do not slay us, Indra; do not forsake us: do not steal away
the joys we cherish.
        —*Rig Veda,* Mandala 1, hymn 104

The anaphora is striking, but rhetoric
is beside the point in such fervent pleading
of helpless people, given life's chances.
We put aside their despair to admire the trope,
for words, even of prayer, are decorative.
They want to avoid catastrophe, to feed
and breed, and sometimes forget to be afraid
when they have enjoyed good luck for a little while.

Our connoisseurship can seem to soar above
experience and the randomness of being,
but the air is too thin. Down here at least
we can breathe when we don't hold our breath
as we muddle along, beset on every side
by perils only some of which we can see.

FOB

The initials hang in the mind
as the crates and bales they describe dangle in air
during the lading. At that precise moment,
as Lord Devlin remarked, only lawyers
could watch "with satisfaction the spectacle
of liabilities shifting as the cargo
sways on the end of the derrick over a notional
perpendicular from the ship's rail."

Giddily apt. Balancing up there,
profit and loss pendulate this way
and that, while from the advocate's POV
(he stands nearby on the dock, gazing upward)
the cosmos displays its sudden quantum leaps
that change from what was one thing to another.

NO MAN IS A HERO TO HIS VALET

Not every hero has a valet, although some valets are heroes.
No man is an island on which everyone is either a hero or a valet.
Heroes' valets can be a convenience to biographers.
No biographers are heroes. And few of them have valets.
Some heroes have batmen, who are military valets.
Batman had a valet, but his tailor was a lunatic.
Some lunatics have valets—loyal ones who stayed on
        after their masters went mad.
Those valets are heroes.
"Lunatics" is now politically incorrect, but people with valets
        still use the word.
Most people with valets know how to pronounce the word.
Was Rudy Vallée's name really Rudy Valet?
"Unless my valet winds my watch and puts it on my wrist,
        I have no idea what time it is."
"You could look at your phone, you twit."
Many twits have valets, who serve mostly to be amused.
The twits don't know this, or, if they do, don't care.
Which makes them heroes, in a way.
But not to their valets.

AZRAËL

A familiar stranger, you see him now and then
at a bus stop or in line at a checkout counter.
Neither you nor he has felt the need
to acknowledge each other's presence or presume
even to exchange first names. But you
have made your guess: that he is Azraël
and you avert your eyes and keep your distance.
Has he noticed you? He never smiles
or nods. Or not yet. You tell yourself
that this is merely a fancy. But if not?
You know who he is and what his job is,
and all you can hope from him is that because
he's seen you around he may treat you gently.

NOTHING ON MY MIND

Meditate; empty the mind; become
stupid to learn what the stupids have always known
(although they may not have been aware that they know it).
Then go beyond stupid to its perfection:
the stupor of dirt and mute stones—nature.

A poem about nothing, or essay or novel,
would be blank pages, the grain of the paper
disdaining ink and its awkward compromises.

Close your eyes and you will perhaps see,
or think you see, beyond the eye's limit
and then the mind's limit. You have always
suspected that whatever there is is there.

To cozy up to nothing can be useful:
you must learn not to fear it, or fear it less.
You achieve a state of denial most of the time
as you try to avoid the one sure thing
every one of us faces. A man's estate
is what he leaves behind him, what he had
and had to let go. It devolves then to his heirs
and comes once again to nothing—as they discover.

Wealthy men in India in old age
exchange their accustomed luxury to wander,
taking with them only a beggar's bowl.
In the West we marvel at them and sometimes wonder
whether they can see what is coming and practice
to accustom themselves to the nothing that awaits them
and to tame terror to bearable unease.

Less than nothing cannot be worse than nothing.
Negative numbers are constructs like dark matter
and exist in a limbo. Does Limbo still exist?
Fra Rainaldo da Piperno said that
the Limbo of Infants is an eternal state
of natural joy, untempered by any sense
of loss at how much greater their joy might have been
had they been baptized, a statement as vague
as the state itself. For theologians now,
it is not quite a doctrine, but not quite not.
The idea, too, is in limbo, a "permitted opinion."

The speed of darkness must equal the speed of light:
as light makes its way, darkness recedes,
and as light disappears, darkness comes to replace it.

Adept monks can meditate in the darkness
of the deepest caves carved into the mountain.
Do they close their eyes and then imagine
the black that surrounds them, even though it is there?
Or are their eyes open that might be closed?
They do not worry about such things but think
empty thoughts, or so I like to suppose.

Can you believe your eyes? What you can see
means nothing; what you imagine or think
also means nothing. Nihil obstat.

MUSHROOMS

The poison in a mushroom does it no good.
It doesn't know, nor does the fellow who eats it,
but he will find out. And maybe he will tell
others about the mushroom and even describe it,
a death cap, say. Others of that species
are beneficiaries, and other kinds
because people will hesitate unless
they're sure that what they are eating is safe. The death
of the one (mushroom, I mean, not the man)
may save the others. And what greater love
than to give one's life to save a fellow mushroom?
Or does that go too far? Take into account
the sweet revenge the mushroom anticipates
jouncing along in the basket. Destroying angels
could take the same satisfaction—but that is assuming
mushrooms think and are self-aware. Unlikely,
so we are forced to look up to a practical-joker
God who, having thought of this intricate business,
couldn't resist. Mushrooms seldom laugh
but He does, often, at his cruelest jokes.

QUI VIVE

Sea serpents, land serpents, insects,
certain frogs and fish, a number of plants,
and microscopic vectors that everywhere
deliver poison to those who are arriving
and those who are leaving: we cannot escape them.
They argue among themselves—which is the worst,
the fastest killer, the slowest, the one that inflicts
the most pain. . . . But who can blame them? They do
what they have to do and know how to do, proud
of performing their assignments well. The Vedic
hymn describes their world, or the state of mind
that makes it our world, whether or not
we admit it. Poems, like cabbage whites,
flutter while prayers move in straight lines,
as we try to understand and even accept
who and what we are.
                              I lie in the darkness
and feel the flow along my nerves of venom's
toxins, proteins and peptides that still burn
from bites I thought had healed of my black-mamba
memory's fangs—offenses and shortcomings.
Look up at the sand dune's contrasty ridges.
Can you see among the striations the horned vipers
concealed in that painful glare? You have to stare
with the keen eyes of a predator or prey.
I think of those tiny creatures that scamper, silent,
in darkness from one hiding place to another,
eyes peeled and ears pricked in terror.
They live at a pitch we do not have to imagine.
Even in a terrarium, safe, their instincts
tell them to crouch near the artificial rock
they do not understand is decorative.
(Breath follows nervous breath, and who has the time
or even the inclination to decorate?)

A prospect of death concentrates the mind.
It should work for us as it does for mice and gerbils.
Poisons are, by definition, ingested
while venoms are injected (few victims
worry about the distinction). We're also hosts
to threats of hunger and thirst we fight forever,
for if they persist over a length of time,
they kill as surely as any pharmacist's secret
compound. Not even relative safety is safe.
We remain on the qui vive—but for whom do we wish
that long life? A wrong answer will kill you,
getting you hacked with a halberd or thrown down
into the moat in which there are probably not
those crocodiles the peasants speak of, but still
the drop is long enough to break your neck.
Neanderthals along the Dordogne's banks
waited for the reindeer coming to drink
and whenever they were feeling a bit peckish
would kill one and eat it. They had comfort,
leisure, and luck and could take up painting—aurochs,
horses, and bulls—starting civilization
as they ventured beyond needing to mere wanting,
where most of us live now or think we do.
Still, there are men and women who fear spiders,
mice, bats, toads, and snakes, their instincts
stronger than their reason can justify.

TANGO

If a Jew learns the tango, is he still
a Jew? Probably not Orthodox,
but the rest of us still share some disinclination.
We may play tennis, baseball, football even,

and climb mountains; we perform in jazz bands
(or did when there were jazz bands); but this dance,
blatant concupiscence, celebrates
the sorrows of the flesh to music nothing

like the song which is Solomon's. Klezmer doesn't
cut it. I listen to tangos with eyes closed
and see the *trayf* world outside the law
that some of us allow ourselves to long for.

ARBORICULTURE

Birds soar overhead or dart
among my branches. Sometimes one
may perch for a moment on one of my twigs,
but then take off. There have been times
when a pair would nest and stay for a season
but they were temporary, guests
and not, as I'm tempted to think, me.
I take no credit for them—whims,
fleeting if diverting fancies.
I study stolidity, as wood
should, and how to be content.

LA VALLÉE D'OBERMANN

Doesn't exist, except in the moody music
of Liszt's *Année,* so it isn't where the dogs
come from or Louis either, who first bred them,
but the Jura should have such places, isolated

and with *un profond sentiment de tristesse,*
not far from Kitsch, perhaps, that tourist mecca
where shopgirls dress in traditional native costumes
and the weather is always lovely. One can look up

from writing postcards at a café table
to contemplate the fountain pen's mountain looming
in the cloudless azure sky. Far to the north,
Isigny in Normandy deigns to be real

but lacks talking ducks, mice, and pigs,
unless you bring them with you (as many do).
The question remains: where was Louis from,
or, strictly speaking, his people? A long line

of prison guards and executioners? Farming
is tough there and they had to support themselves
somehow in that *mauvais milieu.* They could always
plow or shovel snow or try to get by

making crude gloves with cat-fur linings
or cleaning each other's wretched cottages:
unfettered by existence, in limitless freedom,
people are not likely to be more attractive.

EDEN

All this kvetching about how we were expelled
from Eden is self-absorbed, unworthy of even
former residents. Think of the implication—
that Eden, at the same time, lost itself
and without us was degraded, too, no longer
what it had been, but now just a garden
(nice if you like landscapes, but unimportant).
Or else it was diminished to mere idea

(God's or ours?) that we sometimes invoke
to beat ourselves up—and therefore, a bad idea.
Those are like weeds, hardier than you'd think,
considering that they are all wrong. But weeds
are simply plants improperly sited, or ugly,
or hallucinogenic, the bitter buds of the truth.

GARBO'S CAT

For Nina

I awoke this morning to discover that I could understand Cat—
not speak it but I knew what her different mews meant.
And she told me how her great-great-aunt Agrippina had as her caretaker
Greta Garbo. The star once brought home a new lover
only to find that the woman was allergic to cats.
Sneezing, eyes tearing, and a rash on her face and neck.
An unfortunate look altogether. The woman apologized
but said that either she or the cat would have to go.
Out of the room if not the entire apartment.
Garbo thought for a moment and announced that the cat would stay.
"But why?" her maid asked her the following morning.
"Both of them are beautiful," Garbo answered,
"but the cat never says anything stupid."

PARADIGMS OF VERBS

Cats do not need subjunctives—other moods
are of no interest to them. And personal endings
of verbs are beneath their notice: what difference
does it make who did what, whatever it was?
The present tense is all they know: it's always
now (and for minutes ago the historical present
serves perfectly well). The rest of grammar
with which we take such pains is mostly distracting
from what is before our eyes in the wink of which
we risk missing the point. That may be why
cats do not have to blink, an adaptive advantage.
In a trance that holy men aspire to,
stare fixedly at what you can see
until your vision clears to the singular
and visionary. Your life depends upon it.

COMFORT FOR MOURNERS

In the end, it is grammar that saves us, encompassing
everything that happens or has happened
or will happen with tenses' eternal distinctions.
What the present no longer holds slips into
a past where there are no more movements, no more
vicissitudes. It is comfortable there in a silence
we cannot imagine, a haven or say a heaven,
unlike this world that skeptics can believe in.

The future is aspirational; the present,
infinitesimal. There are only the past,
perfect, and pluperfect stretching behind us,
and the rule of subordination of tenses applies,
will, does, and did, time without end.

THE GNU

You cannot train the tapir
to go upon the paper,

as you can do
with a gnu.

OLD SNAPSHOT

A photograph on the desk of my father and me
on a beach somewhere in bathing suits: he
wears one of those antiques that has a vest
above the trunks. I am three I guess.

Sunlight comes in through the window an hour a day
to shine on the picture so that it's fading away.
I ought to move it, but don't because it shows
how a memory over time will lose

definition. It takes on a ghostliness
the one with the Kodak (my mother, I would guess)
could not have imagined. I think of the eerie way
we came into being in the developer tray.

Now we reverse so our figures begin
to retreat into the white paper and in
time deliquesce to a mere idea of what
we were once when the box camera caught

that instant from which we are being freed in the slow,
daily assault of sunlight through which we go.
In time we shall float away from our last ties
to earth. And my father will hold me as we rise.

THE RIGHT TO OBLIVION

Mostly it's Google's problem, but the French
assert it, because fame doesn't last and shouldn't.
There's a privacy right for a man, hero or villain,
to return in time to his obscure place
in the herd, unnoticed and indistinguishable.
Google's trick therefore becomes invasive
and ever more unnatural. Books are, too,
even if they are relegated to storage

for falling below some circulation level.
Bref: unless almost everyone knows it,
for any of us to repeat (or even to know)
any dusty fact may be offensive.
Whatever people are ignorant of cannot
disturb their received ideas or stir up trouble.

FOR JANET ON HER BIRTHDAY

The rocks, the white water, the treacherous falls
are behind you now and the river broadens to
a tranquil smoothness momentary squalls
can ruffle temporarily, but you

know they will soon subside, having learned
the tricks of the winds and the current. Your prospects are
excellent. You can tell when the tide has turned:
the inlet and the cove cannot be far.

This is the best part of the trip and is worth
whatever went before. Your vessel is strong,
shipshape as the day it left its berth.
Relax and enjoy yourself as you float along.

ANSWER

I cannot guess the answer. The question also
is less than clear, but I am uneasy that one
is pending in the interrogative air

we have some sense of—will it rain or snow?
We can tell despite the clear blue sky
and often we turn out to be right. So, here;

so, now. A presence of absence, a difficult
thing like negative space. It is not a vacuum
but a lower pressure to which the nerves respond.

I cannot rack my brain. I have to relax
to allow for the neurons' inklings I may imagine.
Is that a kind of knowing? Or even a hint?

Patience may not clarify, but what
choice is there? Those in the business venture
answers that may be relevant or not,

and there is some satisfaction in replying
to fanciful queries, to problems never posed.
A thunderstorm, clearing, will leave a trace

of ozone: this is like that, something off
that the nerves can apperceive. Do they belong
to the body or the mind? Are they double agents,

and more to be trusted or less? Far too refined
and even silly, these cannot be the questions.
Think of scampering animals suddenly stopping,

having received a message from some sense
we have forgotten we have that warns of danger.
The creature, perhaps the species, depends upon it.

We are the ones who doubt; we can afford to,
but that only makes us poorer. All I know
about the question is that there is one,

and any answer will satisfy for a while
but the feeling will come back. Is that the answer?
Probably not the right one. Pencils down.

TORNADO

On the news, a ruined house: beside it,
one the storm spared—not a shutter disturbed.
Do they underline each other or mock each other?
The reporter doesn't think to address such questions,

but there must be a meaning, meanings on both sides
of the property line its whim toed and made real.
It was over in seconds. Does that at all diminish
what happened here but not there? The air

then went silent; the sky turned blue; and the menace
was gone, an invisible wave in a tranquil sea.
A riddle, except that the answer is not clever—
that reason fails and gravity has limits.

On to sports, commercials, a promo. The eye
ambles on, but for them, whose houses
were or weren't destroyed, time froze
and their lives were fixed forever as witnesses

to the one, true thing they knew but did not
understand. Beyond the limits of wisdom
where envy, rage, and relief swirl together
to stain the deceptive sky above their heads,

light shrivels and forgets itself,
ruined and dark as a coffin lid, and the glare
is blinding as that shriek of the wordless wind
is deafening: the end of the end of the world.

On the one side, the eternal idea that cannot
be touched and the painful and fading memory;
on the other, the physical thing, solid but fragile,
aspiring, but doomed to perpetual failure.

Neither is where you'd want to settle in,
but you have no choice. Wherever you are, you find
yourself and contrive to live but with great caution,
shifting with every step from left to right.

CLOSED CAPTIONS

say what the actors will say before they say it.
Their characters said it first, or the writer really,
but now I know seconds in advance
the words they will speak. This makes the encounter
of lovers, say, a scene, a piece of performance

[which it could have been, but that's another poem].
What I observe therefore is the actor's talent:
How will he deliver the line I've read?
The way I expected, or somehow better than that—
better if he's good. The captions below him

turn us all into critics—a risky business,
because the movie will end but the appraising
eye will never close. I cannot change
the words, the gestures, the blocking all around me,
but afterwards I will have notes for them all.

THE QUEST OF SIR MOTL

What vertue is so fitting for a knight,
Or for a ladie whom a knight should love,
As curtesie, to bear themselves aright
To all of each degree, as doth behove?
—*The Faerie Queene*, Book VI, Canto ii, 1

On a field Gules, quartered by two stars
Or, six-pointed, and, below the bordure,
the motto: NEVERTHELESS. Is it Sir Motl
or one of his minyan minions?
Who knows? They keep to themselves, these Jews,
wary that what has happened to them before
could happen again. They have learned to expect it.

Just out of sight, obscured by a *laurier*
of the *Faerie Queene* or *Orlando Furioso,*
Motl waits (or should we say he "lurks"?)
in case some goyish knight on his quest should stop
to ask directions in this dark, anagogic
wood. Not for nothing did those bold
adventurers refer to themselves as "errant."
The knights, although not all benighted, were hardly
well equipped for ratiocination.
The clever ones—there must have been a few—
hid their lights under a bushel or pail
or closed helmet, whatever was at hand.
Trial by combat, for instance, is imprecise,
addressing as it does the wrong question;
and even with its point a long lance
without a token of words remains pointless.
Up on your high horse, you can get hurt,
can get your head knocked off. (Come down from there!)
Sir Motl says he's sorry and promises never
to do such a thing again. But NEVERTHELESS

glows as bright in his heart as on his blazon.
A vague thought has value if it gives rise
to another better or at least clearer thought
that, like a phoenix, rises from its ashes,
announced by that modest, syncategorematic
adverb. Subjects and objects swirl in the world's
welter and cannot hold our flighty attention
as do the grammar's steel-hard filaments.

At Motl's byword we perk up, eager
to hear how the revision or qualification
can focus a flabby verb, so the sentence rings
like crystal flicked by a skeptical fingernail.
Motl has other, more immediate problems,
which is why he hides beneath his heraldic tree.
Above him flies a jessed falcon that figures
an idea crossing high in the empty sky
of a vacant mind. Listen, its bell tinkles,
a sound you would miss if you were paying attention
to anything else and less important. Our deafness,
denseness, and dimness are, we confess, our nature,
to admit which may not quite be the beginning
of wisdom but is at least its precondition.
(Honesty gives us a peek a few lines ahead.)

Because they are on a quest, the knights and squires
have to ask where they are. Motl knows
better, for going nowhere, you cannot get lost.
A purpose, even purposiveness itself
is delusional. How can a cockroach, fleeing
the light, enlighten us about ideation
except that we ought not to attribute to it
too much? Sir Motl's cautious answer
is never to offer answers and thus avoid
mistakes. If some of these slow, metal-clad
pomposities interpret a nod of his head
as a hint at orientation, that's their business.

Better that they should stop and ask themselves
if there is or ever was a grail.
All those other knights, searching for years
(not untold but told and retold) came back
embarrassed and empty-handed. Why don't they go
and find their own grove and a tree to sit under?
And anyway why would one want a grail?
Eternal youth? (If you had it, you would learn
what a burden it is and undertake
another quest to rid yourself of it.)

There they are in a tapestry on the wall
and only Merlin and maybe his sister can see
the invisible threads on the back and hazard a guess
as to what they might mean—a forest scene
fading and ever more difficult to interpret.

Sir Motl has heard all those *chansons de geste*
(de jest?) and knows this, too—not just because
he is a Jew but because he is standing still
in the one place under the one tree
as was the Buddha's practice: it worked for him,
as many people believe. Anything else
is superfluous, decorative, but distracting.
Quests, simple, demand simplicity.

You will not find him in study guides.
Editors are embarrassed and publishers
fear protests and lawsuits. Motl agrees,
there is no need: students will face the world's
crude lesson plan to discover what Eliot meant,
(and Pound, and Hemingway, and Dickens, too,
and Trollope). The dullest dullards who've never read
any books have got the clear message—
that we are different, therefore frightening,
and therefore hateful. The tapestry's artful stories
were clear enough in cartoons. Still we need

reminders, and Motl's appearance, violating
the laws of time and space, accomplishes that.
These knights are not our friends. They hate dragons,
wizards, and Jews, too, but not all the time.
We thus grow complacent and come to trust them.
Does the Redcrosse Knight not condescend?
Are Guyon's good manners mere veneer?
The crucial moments come too late to reveal
the truth. Motl's reserve they take as a sign
of his duplicity (although authentic
after his long history of hurts).

Sir Guyon? You remember (or maybe not):
the champion of Temperance—and who
can disapprove of that? His steed's name
is Brigador (the name now of a game).
He fights an ugly hag and a madman, Furor,
who "workes much shame and woe" on any knight.
The hag as we discover is Furor's mother,
whose vile insults Guyon has to silence
before he fights (fights back) against the son.
Given the limits of Spenser's imagination,
Guyon pulls out her tongue which he then locks
with an yron lock . . . (Does he bring these along
for such occasions, tools of his odd trade?)
[Such impertinent questions slow the action.]
Sir Motl raises them quietly: his weapons
are subtle and harder for knights to defend against.
He is not merely intelligent, though that helps,
but has a sense of humor, which is how Jews
have learned to cope with the alien cultures around us.
His reticence allows for interpretation:
is he trying to blend into the surround
or does he plan to participate somehow?
For a while, either strategy seems to offer
a possible way to proceed and a minimal safety,
but neither of them works for long. The weather

sooner or later changes, as weather will.
Consider Spain or Poland, not to mention
Germany. Look at New York, where our guard
has been down. Suppose we could speak to Motl.
What would he say or advise us to do, except
to keep our bags packed? (We all know this,
having been told often when we were children.)

Even if you have yet to schottische through
the whole epic, you know Sansfoy, Sansloy,
and Sansjoy, Edmund's eminent stooges.
(Sansloy is the one who kills Una's lion
and then tries to rape her.) They disappear
somewhere along the way. Sir Motl does not
bother to distinguish but distrusts them
all, having witnessed through generations
the bloody squabbles of Christians against Christians
whose beliefs differ only minutely. (As long
as they fight among themselves, will they leave us alone,
quiet in the heart of our somber grove?)
A risky plan, but what else is there? Reason
never does any good. Have you tried to talk
with one of these want-wits? Lancelot's little mind
wanders. Percival sports a forbidding scowl
that makes him appear to be paying attention,
but, no, that's his expression when he chooses
between a couple of apples. Agravain
uses his fingers to count; he still has trouble
adding, while subtraction is beyond him
and in his frustration he can lose his temper.
Better to keep still and out of sight.

In dreary prosaic combat the winners are often
the prudent ones, who, smart, never show up.
NEVERTHELESS, we read these poems, to pass
as one of them. (And the time.) Poems could be
of use if more of those pretentious Christians

(and atheists) read them—even assigned. (But who
takes those courses now? Are they still offered?
Does the graphic novel count?) Sir Motl
hides in part because his adversaries
do not deserve an encounter. He has to admit
that his imposture turns real when Galeshin's
arrogance begins to seem comfortable.
Motl compares himself to the trapdoor spider
awaiting one of its luscious moments. Its life,
although not adventurous, can be long:
biologists record that one of the species
survived for forty-three years, its kind's Nestor.

The appeal to nature, however, comes with problems,
for we do not know much about nature and cannot
even frame intelligent questions. Under
dense foliage, motionless, Motl knows
enough to know how little he knows. He keeps
his thoughts to himself where they stay put as he does,
balancing safety and risk. On the duff at his feet,
dapples of sunlight dance while the wind toys
with the verdure overhead. There is no pattern
but only tantalization, for how can you tell
what you do not know from what cannot be known?
A slight breeze from the east, not having been sent
to cool his face, does so nonetheless.

The declarative sentences of consciousness
are clear enough but can be misleading without
their qualifying clauses, refining thoughts,
the beginnings of reason, where an opaque landscape
begins to shimmer into what passes as meaning.
You do not trust your eyes, but how can you doubt
your mind? Do shadows themselves beget shadows?
We thus distract ourselves from the one true thing
which is fear of what may at any moment emerge
from the bosky dell—monster, wizard, or dragon,

fire-breathing, of course. (Do they cauterize
and brutally cure, assuming you live through it?
No, but that would refresh these tired legends.)

Days go by, weeks in which nothing happens,
but Motl, in his enemies' absence, fights
with memories, his own or secondhand,
replaying painful and, worse, shameful scenes,
and attacking himself, unmoving and silent,
repeatedly. Sometimes he alters the outcome,
but never convincingly. The light changes
and what he sees is cruel parody
or offensive burlesque. (Recognizing the genre,
a heartless diagnosis, does not diminish
the hurt he feels, faithful and familiar,
although the scars sometimes transform themselves
to persist as itches, another mode of pain.)

Guyon battles Furor (wins, of course)
and binds him hand and foot. His yron teeth
he gnashes grimly (what other way is there?)
and shoots from his burning eyes sparkes of fyre.
Literature! But over the years details
of rhyme and meter, where a poem lives,
fade to leave behind garish fragments,
sharp shards of unpleasant dreams, absurd
but less and less—and harder to dismiss.
Or think of reading a text in a foreign language
you have mostly forgotten but still can guess
the gist. (What more do we know of our waking lives?)

English is and is not his native tongue
but he speaks it well enough to feel its temptation,
which is why he hides, spying on strangers
(strange at least to him as he to them).
The contempt to which he surely is entitled
shreds, frays here and there, and he is exposed

to biting winds he fears he must deserve.
His few friends, a skewed group, share
his isolation from noblemen and peasants.
But does he never wonder whether the cause
is in his Jewishness or in himself?
(And which would he prefer if he could choose?)
He once considered a change of name: Motl?
A yellow star of David. Moritz, maybe?
Maurice? Marcel? Can improbability serve
as punctuation? "Wink! Wink!" with a complicit
grin. So Motl kept his given name.

The threats are never obvious. These knights
are too silly to fear, as Spenser is.
What Motl cannot resist is spying upon
the hostile world. He is charmed by its music.
Why not? What harm? It is mathematics really
that means and doesn't mean, abstract and clean.
The melodies are seductive, but the damage
is in the continuo line you cannot help
following, singing along with, silently
taking part and owning it, until
you find that it owns you. No grove is safe,
as long as your memory sings what isn't yours,
even though you'd prefer silence. Fugues,
two- and three-part inventions, intricate canons. . . .
Neutral, surely. But listen, Motl, consider
what comes next: magnificats, requiems,
and stabat maters while, just down the street,
almost next door, at the new opera house,
pieties in costumes of melodrama
offer the same message, but simplified,
and certainly not ours. And Christmas carols
are everywhere, relentless, from Thanksgiving
or sooner, like the gaudy decorations.
A cheap shot? But such drops wear away
hard stones and over time can transform

the topography, digging their channels into
soft gray matter. (And whom do you call
to exterminate earworms?) Worst of all,
what you learn to love, what you think improves you
is poison to who you are, or used to be.
Motl would call you a *feinschmecker* of *trayf.*

Nonetheless, there's Dante's imaginary
chum Virgil, his guide with an unlikely
facility in Italian, lingo and culture. . . .
(Remember they're all dead down in hell
and can speak however the poet orders them to.)
He's Motl's antecedent, emblematic
of the unity of mankind, pagans and Christians,
Guelphs and Ghibellines, Arezzo and Florence
all good neighbors, companionable cousins—
a preposterous idea, which is concealed
in a pleasant rosiness one must allow for
in the suburbs of the City of God—Dante's
gift, not to be realized but longed for
and dreamt about, in which painful case
the dream sours into an accusation.
[The gifts of poets are often complicated.]
Let us imagine, then, because we can,
a conversation between the two hierophants,
surprised to be introduced to each other, but not
astonished (or if so they do not show it).

Do they speak in Latin? Vilna Yiddish? English?
Or exchange thoughts without the constraints of grammar
and words (which is where poets long to live)?
A ridiculous and possibly vital question,
but it excuses me from the need to contrive
dialogue as Motl and Virgil go
right to the unembellished message that poets
avoid (not me but Dante's Virgil and Motl—
who is much less well-known because I am).

They agree that there is a culture on which they rely
but cannot swallow whole: they stand aslant,
in harmony sometimes, but dissidence, too,
as the occasion prompts. From the outside
everything looks different. (Motl's kinfolk,
Freud and Marx, explained the world to the Gentiles
that they could never otherwise have imagined.)

More than I can suggest, their talk glitters,
as good conversation always does, with grace notes,
playful inflections, setups and witty payoffs
to disguise, if only for good manners' sake,
any excessive earnestness. It should seem
cleverly impromptu, a thing of the moment.
Would Virgil have endorsed the Catholic model
of the universe, that eschatological sci-fi,
naive if somehow charming? And would Sir Motl
find it difficult not to laugh aloud,
hidden away in his grove where the knights errant
on their pointless quests pass this way and that?

So where are they, these two, what locus-focus
can we adduce for them? They are in my head,
which is, as always, my subject. Or more precisely
its deformities that define me. My ideas
were never my idea but rather happened,
fortuitous conjunctions I mistook
as significant. How, after all, do Spenser
and Dante relate to me or I to them?
Did it ever help me to know that Vanni Fucci
and two friends (both also named Vanni)
in 1293 stole various treasures
from the sacristy of the cathedral of Pistoia?
It would be (and was) on the midterm exam
in Thomas Bergen's course. We had to ignore
the poem but memorize the footnotes. Loony?

Pozzo! As was the entire enterprise.
Early on, children learn to accept
the irrational and the absurd. (I am still learning.)

The hardest part of introducing students
to poetry is the poetry, which you cannot
begin to talk about. If they gots to ask,
they never gets to know—an inconvenient
pedagogical truth nobody mentions.
But that is what seduced me—the beguiling
shiksa. And I was hardly the first. Think
of Karl Shapiro and Delmore Schwartz. (I knew them
both and they hardly seemed like guardian angels.
But go know! Angels like to play dress-up.)
These days, Jewish poets writing in English
are three for a shekel but these—Karl and Delmore—
were the pioneers. Back then, serious men
(mostly men, and not what you'd call sexists)
discussed at a faculty meeting at Bryn Mawr
the idea of a Jew in the English department.
Many of them argued that while the subject
was literature and language, it also included
the civilization, the attitude, the shirts
bespoke from Savile Row by the half dozen.
(For some years, my grandfather made those shirts.)
What they were teaching was what it means to be English,
and how could a Jew know this or impart it?
(What about Disraeli? Motl shakes
his head and whispers to me to shut up.)
And did they say "Jew" or, being polite,
avoid the word that sounded to them like an insult?
"Hebrew" because it was less blunt was nicer
and Niceness is part of Englishness—or was
back in the fifties. The candidate (his name
escapes me) was better prepared than they could imagine:
his distance was clarifying and would have been helpful.

Who could better understand and define
Gentile Studies? You don't have to be Greek
to teach Thucydides. Motl is silent,
but look closely. Is he suppressing a smile?

So what do they talk about, Motl and Virgil?
After Signor Alighieri's fancy,
fanciful flight, Virgil wants to avoid
religion this time and find something congenial.
To signal this disinclination, he nudges Motl
toward more trivial truths about which wars
are seldom fought: a god, he says, to foreclose
further blather, is anything that can kill you.
What more need be said? Motl agrees:
Jupiter, Cupid, Augustus, plague, the Goths,
whatever you fear or discover you ought to have feared.
Now they can turn to the more important things—
music, sculpture, painting, favorite wines,
and, with an outstanding kitchen staff,
witty deserts with which one can show off.

Both of them are civilized enough
not to talk about work—or poetry.
You understand their reticence. . . . Or do you?
Rabbis discuss Torah, Talmud tractates,
and other such subjects and are not embarrassed.
For pious Jews there are no distractions.
Outside the study house is nothing important
or nothing at all, until it has been ordered,
decoded, and clarified by the books and scrolls,
those relics of Eden spread out on tables before them.

Does Motl sometimes look out of the window
at shadows floating past on the Polish snow?
I do, and there's Nabokov, there's Calvino.
And Faulkner. Auden, maybe? Probably Yeats.
We peer into darkness and see our faces reflected

in the windowpane: on both sides is loss.
I admit I sometimes envy those *haredim*
who know who they are, have no doubts, are content. . . .
But I cannot join them. If light is both a wave
and a particle, then the world is a pudding
in which nothing is sure or firm. The Cartesian
assertion should have been more modest: *I*
doubt; therefore I am. Doubt, after all,
is what separates us from the lower orders.

Guyon has hardly managed to catch his breath
when he (and Motl and readers, also) "spyde
a vartlet running towardes hastily,
whose flying feet so fast their way applyde,
that round about a cloud of dust did fly,
which, mingled all with sweate, did dim his eye."
Who is he? Why has he come? It doesn't matter.
He's what Macmillan feared: "Events, dear boy,
events." Irrational and unexpected.
Worse still, we realize how our lives
are in a contingent universe—Tohu and Bohu—
from which we believed or imagined we had escaped.
Worst of all, it isn't just that dream
but all of our naive flights to an elsewhere
that doesn't exist. In other words, our childhoods
for the loss of which we have never ceased to mourn.

What Motl likes most is the giddiness
of being neither truly here nor there.
The difficulty would be finding his way
back, if that were his intention. Birds
have eaten the trail of sesame seeds he left
to mark his route's turnings. That dingley dell
he searches for he knows he will never find.
The familiar laurel trees and fleckered light
he longs for and to see and in its fallen leaves
find comfort if not truth. It's quiet, but . . .

too quiet. Whatever the mood of the natives,
he is restless, accustomed to constant menace
of predators everywhere. How does one learn
to distinguish with any certainty drums from thunder?
Savage beasts, doing whatever they do
and have been bred to do are innocent,
but men, duplicitous, are dangerous.

Whatever the point, this would be beside it.
The only choice we have is between Dante
and Petrarch or, further back in Augustus's time,
Virgil and Ovid. The Mantuan, looking back,
might have preferred to be more like Mr. Naso,
who understood that jokes can be a path
to subtle kinds of wisdom. (And we should expect
a subtlety that engages our attention.)
Sir Motl, as I remember, was recalling
that laurel grove in which we first found him,
even though he concedes that it was foreign.
Nostalgia is not an emotion for Jews to indulge in.
Which nostos, after all? Or ask how many
we can feel, layered like a cake.
The wandering Jew is a sad, familiar figure,
but the stable Jew, with roots that sprout from his toes
and work their way deep into the soil,
even through underlying schist and gneiss?
Motl sometimes prefers that sad idea.
I have also played with it now and again,
but it is a dangerous toy with sharp edges
and difficult to resist. When we were children,
who never thought of himself up on a horse,
suited in shiny armor? Not to admit this
would be a betrayal of Motl, who has been patient,
waiting on us, although he would rather hide.
His home is in the shadows, any shadows
where, with everything possible, nothing is real.

TRANSLATIONS,
TRANSFORMATIONS,
ADAPTATIONS

LONGING

AFTER THE YIDDISH OF LEYB NAYDUS

In a torment of terrible dreams, night after night,
I longed for you as a moored sailboat longs
for a puff of wind and the river's cool current;
as the soft curl of a woman's hair can long
for a flower; as the clear blue sky longs
for the tremor of bells, close or faraway;
as an empty cradle longs for an infant's breath,
the shallow and almost silent breathing of sleep;
as an empty mirror longs for a reflection;
or as any beginning longs for its fitting end.

THE WHIP

AFTER THE YIDDISH OF MOYSHE LEYB HALPERN

Galoots in their muddy boots take over your house,
soil the carpets, and stroll from room to room
as if they were in some backstreet whorehouse:
what is most deeply pleasing is grabbing your whip
and like an offended nobleman beating them,
driving them off like a pack of snarling dogs.

But what good is the whip when the intruders
are blue-eyed blonds, stealing into your soul
to perch and chatter like happy little birds
or playing like small children who paddle in brooks,
splashing with pretty feet in your heart's blood?

MY BODY

AFTER THE YIDDISH OF RACHEL KORN

My body is a tree
reaching toward the sky
and sprouting new green leaves again
in the warmth of each new love.

But my shadow that walks with me
is a shroud made to my measure
that slinks behind or leaps forward
over the waiting grass
and moist earth
in childish play.

NIGHT GUESTS

AFTER THE YIDDISH OF KADYA MOLODOVSKY

A bird one night
knocked with his wings
on my window and door.
"Come in, fine-feathered friend.
I can give you water and bread crumbs.
Be my guest. We share the same fate,
living and dying."

A cat passing by
scratched and scraped with its claws.
"Come in, pussycat, friend of my childhood.
Be my guest. We are both vagabonds,
destined to roam."

A nanny goat came
and knocked with her hooves and butted with her horns.
I said, "Come in, old goat, udderly charming.
Be my guest. I am honored.
We were both destined to be teachers."

Then, one night, a man stood at my door,
and this time I was frightened.
"Who are you?" I asked. "Is that a knife in your hand?
Do you mean to do me harm?"
I locked and barred the door,
fell to the floor, and hid my face in my hands.
The floor was as cold as stone.
From outside the door, I heard his pitiful crooning.

VILLANESQUE

JACQUES GRÉVIN

Relying on old stories poets had spread
of love, I supposed that you had to be feigning
indifference, but the years of our youth were waning...
(I have less patience, now that my cravings are fed.)
Your eyes could wound—although I am not complaining:
I remember those times and how our youth was waning.
I was in agony, as if struck dead.
To think of it now is almost entertaining.
We were surprised that the years of our youth were waning,
but more time is behind us than we have ahead.
We practice moderation, and reason is reigning.
Those years of our youth, relentless, are still waning.

SONNET

ÉTIENNE JODELLE

Mhyrra once seethed in a wild lust
to take her mother's place in the marriage bed,
and Scylla cut the purple lock from the head
of her father—only to earn her lover's disgust.
Arachne claimed that her weaving had fewer mistakes
than Athena's, who punished her for her ugly pride.
When Gorgon became Poseidon's one-night bride,
Athena changed her lovely hair to snakes.

Medea used her magic charms to ensnare
Jason, but then in vengeance and despair,
destroyed Jason's new love, Creusa, with fire.
But you are worse than they were: feeble and old,
you are a whore, a horror, a traitor, a scold,
for Myrrha, Scylla, and all the rest to admire.

A FOUNTAIN

PHILIPPE DESPORTES

This fountain is cold and its water, soft and sweet,
the color of silver. It seems to murmur of Love.
Soft grass greens all around, and alders above
provide a respite of shade from the burning heat.
Zephyr ruffles the foliage and soothes,
whispering gently in its merciful shelter
from the flaming noonday sun in which we swelter.
Beyond it the earth bakes and nothing moves.

Having struggled along on your weary way,
burned with heat and pressed by thirst, you may
pause here for a while in this blessed shade.
Let your discomfort and your intelligence rule you.
Out of the sun, these merciful breezes will cool you,
and your thirst will be quenched by the water's steady cascade.

TWO SONNETS

LOUISE LABÉ

1

O lovely brown eyes, O glances refused,
O repetitive sighs, O tears shed,
O dark night with me alone in my bed,
O dawn that shows the night has been ill-used,
O sorry laments, O relentless desires,
O time lost, O heavy fines disbursed,
O destined evils with which I have been cursed,
O thousand deaths and then infernal fires,

O laugh, O face, O hair, arms, hands, and fingers,
O plaintive lute, O voices of sweetest singers:
so many flames to warm—and burn me, too.
I beg of you, bearing your bright flambeaux
through all my heart's chambers where you go,
how is it that no spark ever touches you?

2

I live, I die; on fire, I drown in the sea;
when I touch flames, my fingers are frostbitten.
Life is both dull and sharp: when I am smitten,
I find the greatest joy in my ennui.
For no reason, I laugh and then I cry;
my transports of delight are mixed with grief;
my happiness runs away. Its visits are brief.
My heart blossoms while I wither and die.

Thus, Love in his inconstancy rules me;
when I anticipate sadness, it is his trick
to put me at my ease—if moderately.

But if I let myself trust him, there will be
a peripeteia, cruel and very quick,
as he hurls me down to the depths of misery.

NIGHTINGALES

BERNARD DE VENTADORN

Trees in the woods, refreshed, resume
their vivid greens as I awake,
unburdened from yesterday evening's gloom
by the nightingale's trills—that by mistake
I took for love songs although heartbreak
is what he was singing of. By whom
had he been spurned? Through my bedroom
window came twitters of his heartache.

And I, despite her show of pride,
swallow and smile, as if it were
a reciprocal love for which I bide
my time, having sworn to wait for her
reciprocation—that will occur
at length if heaven is on my side
and Love's. I pray that God may guide
her heart and make me happier.

Meanwhile I languish in a jail
of her devising, punished, although
I have done nothing wrong. I fail
to understand why she is so
severe—for in my heart I know
that Love will in the end prevail.
My sufferings on this grand scale
will give way to pleasure's glow.

Any wrong she may do me
could become a blessing. I
pray God her sweet kiss may be
my spirit's medicine whereby
I shall revive, for I rely

upon her magnanimity:
she is aware that only she
can harrow my hell and raise me high.

My skittering mind changes its views
hour by hour, but my heart, never.
Steadfast, it does not confuse
love and faith with ideas, clever
as they may be. I shall forever
yearn for the lady, and if she choose
to deny my love, then I shall use
death as the cure of my raging fever,

for if the lady will not yield,
there is a drastic remedy
in the grave's tranquility
where lovers' broken hearts are healed.

DIZAIN

MAURICE SCÈVE

Painters can do snow with a whiteness they
make whiter with a few shadows but there
their talent stops and they cannot portray
cold, which you will not feel although you stare
at the canvas with its snowdrifts everywhere.

I can explain evil but cannot convey
its torments of the soul. What the words say
does not suggest the horror, as of a plague,
the collective wretchedness, the shared despair.
The vivid experience turns abstract and vague.

FROM THE FRAGRANT EAST

PIETRO CARDINAL BEMBO

I

In the fabled, fragrant East beneath a clear,
azure sky, the kind and merciful sun
maintains a steady, pleasant atmosphere
neither too hot nor cold, and everyone
is happy, enjoying himself and his career
in the pursuit of leisure, pleasure, and fun,
conforming to Venus's law there, which requires
a timely satisfaction of all desires.

II

Their only prohibition is to ignore
another person's offer of love. In her great
temples they honor the goddess and adore
her gift of desire—that one should reciprocate.
There is no pressing need for any more
legislation in this tranquil state.
The priests enforce their one and only rule,
to disobey which would be both rude and cruel.

III

If some men fail, it is because their souls
are shy and they deprive themselves of much
pleasure, which is the best of mankind's goals.
These the goddess encourages with such
promptings as she can devise and she enrolls
recruits to her cause with a knowing, tender touch.
It is no surprise that there are few
she cannot rouse to do as she'd have them do.

IV

The goddess appeared one morning to command
two of her trusted priests to undertake
a difficult mission to a distant land
and to do this for her and their devotion's sake.
They were to help the foreigners understand
that in the name of chastity they break
Nature's laws, men's hearts, and also their own,
for they condemn themselves to live alone.

V

"Here all men and women are faithful and I
delight in them. Their hearts are already mine
and they are more than willing to comply
with what I have ordained in my divine
teachings and do not need any sermons by
which you explain to them how to refine
their sensual pleasures to more arcane heights.
They please me as they strive after new delights.

VI

"But imagine, just for argument's sake, that one
of my subjects here may get it into his mind
to renounce pleasure. This is seldom done,
but if it should happen, there would be a kind
neighbor who would persuade this paragon
of foolishness to return to the fold to find
arms that would clasp him and lips for him to kiss.
How could any sane person quarrel with this?

VII

"But far to the west, near the Metaurus's stream,
there are benighted ladies who have not
ever been told that life can be a dream.

Instead, these two, misunderstanding what
I have to teach, abjure all pleasure and seem
to deny their hearts and my divinity, but
you will go as nuncios with your nice
message that love is good and not a vice.

VIII

"One of these women rules a great domain
and the other is her cousin and confidante.
Both of them are pious and refrain
from any thoughts of love with some gallant
admirer who declares that he is in pain
from desire because they have refused to grant
relief, and they'd have women near and far
be as chaste as they have been and are.

IX

"The duchess and her friend Emilia both
are wasting their youth, their green and gladsome years,
which saddens me. I wax, as men say, wroth.
Go, dear friends, and whisper into their ears
that all those things they are at present loath
to do are innocent, healthy, and their fears
are groundless. Try to make them realize
that love's delights are not only sweet but wise.

X

"They admire Lucrece who valued her chastity
more than her life, which I think was absurd
and also vain—for she was defying me
and her own nature. Every stupid word
that moralists prate in their perversity
is wrong and belies the truth that Lucrece erred.
To disapprove of her is not contrarian,
but the error of a first-year seminarian.

XI

"My glory, like a snowbank in the warm
spring sun, diminishes. You two
must put a stop to any further harm
they do to me, and I rely on you
to reason with them gently and with charm,
seducing their minds so they may tread the true
path you set before them, both for their
sakes and for their suitors' everywhere."

XII

In Venus's chariot borne aloft by her fleet
of swans the willing missionaries flew
to Egypt and then the islands of Rhodes, Crete,
and Sicily in celerity coming to
the Apennines. Their journey was complete
at Urbino, where they came down from the blue
skies to frighten all the townsmen as much as
impress them. There, they asked to see the duchess.

XIII

They ask her, "Why do you reject Love's laws
or think it harmful when she brings peace
and harmony to all mankind? Because
you believe Love to be a tyrant? Oh, please!
She is often helpful, as when she draws
your best self out and offers it the release
for which it has been praying night and day.
Admit to yourself the truth of what we say!"

XIV

They tell her of a land where all is grace
and ease and love, and how a person's soul
is purified in such a splendid place,

rejoicing in a taste of heaven, that goal
we all strive toward. "There is not a trace
of pain or sadness, so we may extoll
the glorious universe and celebrate
life's miracles from minuscule to great.

XV

"Love is the seed of every good there is;
it lights the dark, intensifies the light,
and presides over the world. Acknowledge this
and accept the treasures of taste and touch and sight,
as you are honored by Nature's gentle kiss.
Claim with pride and gratitude your right
to live your life and have your measure of
God's gifts to men—not least of them love.

XVI

"Love's domain is the earth, the sky, and the sea
in which the creatures thrive because of her
and in her is all life's futurity.
You have been taught badly and you were
misled by fanatic priests and nuns whom we
see ignoring their own rules: they prefer
to teach the virtues in the hope that you
will do as they say rather than as they do.

XVII

"Look in the mirror and see how your face reflects
Nature's intention, for you have felt the gaze
of admiring men your prejudice rejects
although you are aware of the hot blaze
of passion that makes their eyes shine and expects
nothing in return for the fervent praise
they offer you. They try hard not to stare
but you feel the ardor of their silent prayer.

XVIII

"Our mistress is a goddess and she invites
both of you to join her and learn how
her humane laws offer lovely nights
and delicious days. Come and join us now
where beauty can arouse such appetites
that we must not ignore or disavow.
These gifts are calibrated: there can be
fulfillment that never turns to satiety.

XIX

"It is Love that orders the earth, the sky, and the sea
and fosters the lives of animals and plants.
Over all the visible world, it is she
who rules, imposing order on the chance
and random turmoil of atoms so they may be
solid enough to stand upon and dance.
We wonder at nature's complications and know
how they work because she would have it so.

XX

"But think of those things that come directly from Jove:
the planets in their orbits in the sky
so beautiful above us as they move.
He may have created them all on high
but the virtue that arises from them is Love
by whose benevolence they vivify.
She asperses a sweet and gentle rain
so they can renew themselves and be born again.

XXI

"The finest poets sing your praises and yet
you ignore what they say in their clever
stanzas. You hear their words but you forget

their meaning as you contrive somehow to sever
manner from matter as in some canzonet
in which you can't make out the words, but never
mind, for the tune delights and satisfies.
The bliss you feel within you never dies.

XXII

"Have you never read the engaging verses
of Ovid or Tibullus celebrating
the joys of love or else reciting curses
on those who refuse the wretched lovers waiting
at their gates or doorposts, having sent nurses
with gifts? And what were they anticipating,
uncertain whether the woman would be his
blessing or his terrible nemesis?

XXIII

"In another language and more recently
Cino da Pistoia turned his mind
to love as did great Dante, whom we see
yearning for Beatrice. Although resigned
never to possess the lady, he
made her famous so that even the blind,
hearing his words, can see her lovely face
lit by the warm glow of heaven's grace.

XXIV

"Petrarch, too, showed us all the fair
Laura, whom he adored with his whole heart.
Because of him, her name still floats on the air
generations later. Through the art
of his sonnets men have been taught how to care
for the gift of a woman's presence that is the start
of a spiritual progress by which we
may glimpse the sweetness of eternity.

XXV

"Consider therefore how your beauty has
its effect on men: the villains are improved
and the rude are civilized. If someone was
an utter churl, by your glance he is moved,
refined in everything he thinks and does.
With such a power has it not behooved
you two to mix in the world for kindness' sake
and see the difference you and your loves can make?

XXVI

"All terrestrial excellence that was fated
to show itself beneath the starry sky
and all the beauties time has anticipated
are epitomized in you for the human eye
to see, be filled with awe, and with breath bated
devote itself to the love it is captured by,
understanding it as the affirmation
of life and of the grandeur of creation.

XXVII

"In your cheeks are roses red and white
fresh picked in heaven's garden, and your lips
are rubies with pearls among them. It is a sight
that separates each man from his soul that slips
upward to rejoice in the sun's bright light
as the earth rejoices after an eclipse.
Reason and emotion thus combined
offer the gift of wisdom to man's mind.

XXVIII

"Dismiss the evil thought that steels your heart
against Love's blandishments and causes pain
to those who would be your lovers. Quite apart

from the harm you do to yourselves, it must be plain
that your friends are also hurt. For their sakes, start
setting a good example and as you reign,
take care of your many subjects who follow you
as sheep, their shepherdess in all you do.

XXIX

"Think of your pride as a fountain with its high
jet of water sparkling like jewels
before it falls back into the basin. Why
should you ask questions only knaves and fools
would pose? You will discover by and by
that we are right and that your high-flown rules
aim upward but immediately collapse,
and then you may harken to Love's sweet song perhaps.

XXX

"Listen as well to your many suitors to whom
you have been inhospitable and reflect
how crops in the field cannot come into bloom
unless they are plowed and seeded. Do not expect
any harvest but thorns, thistles, and broom,
and such like weeds that we have learned to reject,
for nature will reclaim it: what was tame
will revert to wilderness for birds and game.

XXXI

"Your beauty is like an orchard in April or May
when the trees blossom and the happy owner strolls
through it, enjoying himself each step of the way,
but he knows that summer will come as the earth rolls
through the seasons. The beauty will decay
and pretty flowers wither, for no one controls
time so that nothing lovely stays,
and he'll leave his orchard's heat for a cooler place.

XXXII

"A person who has riches of untold worth
but hates to spend his money might as well be
a pauper. The boat that stays moored in its berth
will rot there if it never puts to sea.
The sun shines and the moon brightens the earth
for you to use. Otherwise obscurity
is what you're fated for, like a gem that lies
deep in the ground, hidden from all eyes.

XXXIII

"What kind of wicked man would bar the door
to truth and beauty and voices in the air
that beckon to us sweetly and implore
us to enter into a garden where
happiness resides? What could be more
damaging to the handsome and the fair
whose youth fades daily if imperceptibly?
Stare into the mirror and you will see.

XXXIV

"Creation could not have put you here intending
that you would live among mankind with so
lovely a face but loveless—which is offending
yourself and all those others, men who go
through passion's tortures, cruel and never-ending.
Think of your mother, whose persistent 'no'
would have prevented your being. It is desire
alone that renews life with its sparks of fire.

XXXV

"Generosity, we all agree,
is a virtue as surely niggardliness is a vice.
To give of yourselves to lovers then must be

a good thing: to deny them is not nice.
You are the bright sunlight by which they see,
but they are blinded by your self-sacrifice.
Your duty and your inclination thus
combine to advise you how to be virtuous.

XXXVI

"Do not believe those stories old wives tell
of chastity and honor. They are lies
told to young girls so that when we sell
them on the marriage market the asking price
will be a little higher. Does this compel
you to think of yourselves as merchandise?
It is a vulgar idea for dullards and fools
who never think to question convention's rules.

XXXVII

"There have been silly women now and then
who applied those stringent peasant ideas to their own
lives and appeared to be deaf and dumb when men
spoke to them of love. They sat alone
like Penelope who refused again and again
the offers of suitors who wanted her and her throne.
Is that a model you want for yourselves: tears,
weaving, and masturbation for twenty years?

XXXVIII

"Odysseus had his adventures, as any male
is likely to do. Shouldn't the rules be the same,
weighing their characters on an equal scale
for men and women, allotting praise or blame
for similar reasons? You do not have to sail
to exotic islands to play romance's game.
Imagine the delightful peccadillos
you might have with your head on neighbors' pillows.

XXXIX

"Nature and God have given us the need
for Love with its sweet and gentle harmony.
The deity's first commandment was to breed
and multiply. Just look around and see
how the sun turns and the winds proceed
to blow and the rivers most obediently
flow downhill, as they are intended to do.
Natural laws apply also to you.

XL

"When summer comes, the earth turns green but the vine,
if it has nothing upon which to climb, lies
on the ground to languish. It will produce no wine
nor even shade from the hot sun in the skies.
To embrace an elm or poplar is the design
it must obey. And every grape vine tries,
clasping with its tendrils' strong embrace
the tree, to live and prosper in God's grace.

XLI

"The lamb grazing in the green field feels
the ram rutting, butting away nearby;
in the ocean's blue, dolphins frisk and seals
churn the water and toss the white spume high.
Everywhere on earth, nature reveals
herself. Up in the beech-tree you can spy
fluttering swallows cavorting in the air.
You can't deny it or claim that you do not care.

XLII

"What use is it to you in ruling great
cities and living in your palatial rooms
with servants everywhere to anticipate

your every wish? These elegant costumes
of crimson silk and the crest on your golden plate
aim for the sun's splendor. The sweet perfumes
that hang in your bedchambers are rank and poor
if you have to sleep alone. What for?

XLIII

"Who would not have a lover, someone dear,
whose happiness is yours, as yours is his?
Your mood improves whenever he is near.
And there is no dazzling heap of gold that is
so precious as he. The answer is, I fear,
obvious, for it is a simple quiz
(unless he is rude in speech and action and base
in heart and mind, a most deplorable case).

XLIV

"Of what could you dream more fondly than a man
who fears for you and loves you more than his own
life, for he lives only through you and can
flourish only in your gaze? Alone
he envies the little mayfly whose lifespan
is a matter of hours, while we have to postpone
our deaths and that relief from suffering,
the anodyne that only death can bring.

XLV

"How fine it is to feel one's heart go weak
in Love's arms! How exquisite a thing
when two embrace each other as they seek
the rich reward that intimacy can bring!
The icicle in the sunshine seems to leak
diamonds as the clouds are vanishing,
overwhelmed by springtime's burst of joy.
The sweetness of such dreams can never cloy.

XLVI

"One whom Love's bright sparks cannot ignite
is dead, or may as well be. She does not even
know that she is unhappy. Her delight
is in imagining a gloomy heaven.
Here on earth, she is a shadow quite
useless as is flour without leaven.
No lover's eyes are there for her to see
not herself but the person she could be.

XLVII

"Plato tells us that each of us is a mere
half, a being trying to be whole.
We search for the other half and persevere
lest we be deformed in body and soul.
We must combine to make a perfect sphere
in order to attain life's sacred goal.
Conjoin, commingle with another: in this
sweet clasping you will realize perfect bliss.

XLVIII

"Find that other person or you may not
fulfill yourself as you pass your dreary days
alone, while a decent loving man is what
you most want. Think of the harsh ways
an enemy would treat you when he has fought
and won: this you do to yourself. Raise
the siege, open your city gates, and send
your emissaries to welcome a good friend.

XLIX

"Believe me or not. The decision is yours, but time
will seek you out either way. Your lovely hair
will turn white. At night you will hear the chime

of the clock's repetitive blows. In your despair
you'll fight to maintain your beauty, once sublime
but fading every day. In the mirror there
will be a sadness and perhaps an anger, too,
at how you lived and chose what not to do.

L

"I could go on, but such prolixity
would be fatiguing, and as I clear a track,
a dismal possibility nags at me,
that all the vegetation is growing back.
For both our sakes then, I think it would be
well to pause. I'll take another whack
at the subject soon. I promise to return
but I have a hundred Italian verbs to learn."